The following is an adaptation of one of the Twelve Steps in the program of Overeaters Anonymous. It is one person's interpretation and does not speak for the O.A. organization.

I'm asking, God

Do you believe that the God of your understanding created you to be compulsive, or did He create you to be free? Discovering the freedom that comes with turning one's will and life over to the care of a Higher Power is the Step by Step adventure of the Overeaters Anonymous program.

Coming to Step Seven, we find ourselves again in a direct relationship with this Higher Power. We are asking God to remove our shortcomings, everything that is standing in the way of our freedom to fully develop our potential. In Step Six we spent as much time as was necessary to become ready to make this request wholeheartedly. Now we are making it, humbly and sincerely, believing that we are meant to have the freedom of recovery.

Suggested on page 76 of the Big Book of Alcoholics Anonymous is the following Seventh Step prayer:

> "My Creator, I am now willing that you should have all of me, good and bad. I pray that you remove from me every single defect of character which stands in the way of my usefulness to you and my fellows. Grant me strength, as I go out from here, to do your bidding. Amen."*

By this time, we are well aware of what a mixed bag we are

**Alcoholics Anonymous*, published by A.A. World Services, New York, NY. Available through Hazelden Educational Materials.

giving our Higher Power when we give ourselves. We say, "You can have me, God, defects and all. I want you to sort me out, to take away what needs to be eliminated, and to make me useful to You and the people around me." As we give ourselves to God, we seek to have fewer liabilities and more assets.

Do you find it hard to ask for what you want? Do you expect to be given what you would like to have without the necessity of asking for it? Are you afraid to ask for fear the answer might be no? Are you too proud to ask for what you need? (If you believe that if asked, God *will* remove your defects, and this is what's frightening you, then you may need to go back to Step Six. You may not be entirely ready.)

Assuming we are prepared to "talk turkey," let's examine the attitude we need to have in order to humbly ask God to remove our shortcomings.

Assuming implies that the answer is out of our control. Most compulsive overeaters have tended to *demand* things from life, from God, from other people, and from ourselves. If these demands have not been met, we have raged, sulked, complained, retaliated, or given up. Asking is not demanding. Asking God implies a dialogue, not a self-centered soliloquy. When we ask, we leave ourselves vulnerable to the response of our Higher Power. And it may not come in the way we expect or desire or think is best.

To ask God for help is to concede that we are unable to accomplish what we want by ourselves. We are not self-sufficient. The process of our ego-reduction continues. Self-will may kick and scream with varying degrees of intensity. If we are headstrong and like to feel independent, it goes against the grain to ask for anything. For example, some of us may drive miles out of our way because we are reluctant to stop and ask for directions. Any admission of ignorance seems an indication of weakness. How many times have we tried to bluff our way through something because we were too embarrassed to admit that we didn't know how to do it?

But the moment comes when we run out of time and patience. Perhaps after all our bright ideas for fixing the leaky faucet fail, we finally call the plumber before we end up with a flood. The pain we tried to eliminate with various home remedies gets worse, and so we finally go to the doctor. Similarly, when we get sufficiently tired and sore from beating our heads against the brick wall of our character defects, we ask God to please get them out of our way.

Our prayer may go like this: "I don't know as much as I thought I did, God. I thought if I stopped overeating and got thin, all my problems would disappear along with the fat, and I would live happily ever after. I thought if I could just get my husband/child/wife to a psychiatrist who would change the behavior that drives me up the wall, everything would be fine. I thought having enough money would be the answer, but there's never enough. I thought a new job would make life exciting, but I'm still bored."

External changes do not alter the fact that we still have to live with our inner selves. If we are not in harmony with our own needs, outside circumstances will never suit us, no matter how we try to rearrange them.

"It's me who has to change, God. I'm asking You to show me how," we say.

But who wants to be humble?

When we were overeating compulsively, humility may not have seemed relevant or desirable. The word humility itself may have sounded old-fashioned and naive, fine for saints, but impractical in the real world. Many of us grew up oriented to achievement and self-sufficiency rather than to dependence on a Higher Power and obedience to His will.

We didn't want to be humble. We wanted to be high. We ate what we wanted, when we wanted it, and as much as we wanted. This was our way of demonstrating our control over life. Nothing was going to come between us and our satisfaction.

The problem was, it didn't work. The high soon turned into a low, as did the other highs we tried — alcohol, drugs, ego trips, selfish sex, to name a few. Using food to feel high made most of us fat, and even if we were able to avoid the fat, the binges left us depressed and full of self-hate.

The old adage that pride goes before a fall has proved itself countless times in our overeating careers. We think everything is going great. We finally have the situation in hand. We forget that we are compulsive overeaters, and we go slipping right down into a binge. After that, we are very, very low.

Humility may not sound appealing, but experience demonstrates that it is the necessary precondition for recovery. For many of us, admitting that we are powerless over food is the beginning of humility. Much as we have tried to prove that we are not really powerless over food ("Maybe I'm only powerless over certain foods," "Powerless at certain times," "Powerless under certain conditions," etc., etc.), we finally admit that we are powerless over food, period.

In terms of recognizing our inability to control what we eat once we take the first compulsive bite, humility makes physical abstinence possible. In terms of recognizing a similar inability to control our character defects by ourselves, humility creates the kind of spiritual condition in which a Higher Power can work with us and through us. If we allow pride to take over, we fall back into the illusion that we are in control. And we blow it every time — physically, emotionally, and spiritually. We may not *like* the idea of being humble, but there is no other way. We will keep getting beaten down by pride until we become humble enough to ask for help and listen to the answer. Like water, humility seeks the lowest level and, paradoxically, it then becomes a source of strength and nourishment. When we are humble, we are open to a Higher Power that can do for us what self-will cannot.

Each day, one day at a time, we are given a reprieve from our illness. To have this reprieve, it is necessary to maintain the spiritual condition of humility. Then the character defects can be defused. They may never disappear entirely. Like the urge to overeat, the potential remains. But those character defects can remain inactive as long as we are focused on letting a Higher Power govern us, and as long as we do not go back to trying to control our own lives and the lives of others.

Step Seven is a continuation of Step Six. We have become ready to have our character defects removed because we are sick and tired of the chaos and havoc they produce in our lives and the lives of those around us. We are asking a Higher Power to remove our shortcomings, and the only way we can make contact with this Higher Power is by asking humbly. Then, in order to have the defects removed, we need to be humble enough to learn new attitudes and new ways of acting.

One definition of humility is "being teachable." We don't have to wear sackcloth and ashes to be humble, and we don't have to feel inferior. (We are not alone in having defects of character.) What humility means is a realistic view of ourselves which allows us to grow and learn. If we accept the fact that we don't know everything, then we will not be locked into self-destructive patterns of behavior. We can be willing to change if we are not rigid with pride. If we are humble, we will not be afraid to try something new. It is pride which insists on always being right and always having the answers.

Step Seven's prerequisite is humility. Without it, we do not recognize the shortcomings that damage ourselves and others. It takes humility to ask a Higher Power to remove them instead of continuing to try to cope with them in a habitually headstrong way. We cannot demand to have the defects removed. We have to be humble enough to ask. So it is that humility becomes desirable when we see it as a key to our recovery.

> "Indeed, the attainment of greater humility is the foundation principle of each of (O.A.'s) Twelve Steps. For without some degree of humility, no (compulsive overeater) can stay (abstinent) at all. Nearly all (O.A.'s) have found, too, that unless they develop much more of this precious quality than may be required just for (abstinence), they still haven't much chance of becoming truly happy. Without it, they cannot live to much useful purpose, or, in adversity, be able to summon the faith that can meet any emergency."*

**Twelve Steps and Twelve Traditions*, published by A.A. World Services, New York, NY, p. 71. Available through Hazelden Educational Materials. (Words in parentheses have been added.)

Our shortcomings

Everyone has character defects, but the only ones we ask God to remove are our own. One of the reasons overeaters programs work is that they teach us to concentrate on how to change our own thinking and behavior rather than how we might be able to manipulate and control other people. If we let someone else's behavior destroy our emotional equilibrium, we are in trouble, since we are powerless to change that person. What we can do is accept the responsibility for our own reactions and learn how to change them. If we react with anger or pain to what someone else says or does, that is our problem. We own our reactions. That means we can choose to let go of the ones that hurt us.

Over the course of the years, we have probably blamed our compulsive overeating on everybody and everything outside of ourselves. "I was the youngest child in the family and was always rewarded with sweets." "My father didn't love me enough." "I was insecure." "We moved constantly, and I didn't have any real friends." "My job is boring and frustrating." "My wife has lost interest in sex, and so I eat." "My son has dropped out of school." "My mother-in-law came to live with us." "I'm going through a divorce." All marvelous reasons for overeating, we rationalize.

However, if we recall our past objectively, we see that there was always a reason for overeating, and if it hadn't been one thing it would have been another. We overate because we were compulsive overeaters. The deeper we get into the Steps, the more clearly we understand that instead of overeating as a reaction to various problems, it was the other way around. *Because we overate, we created unnecessary problems for ourselves.* We sought in food what we could not realistically expect from life — the satisfaction of all our impulses and desires.

Because we were hooked on overeating, we withdrew from people and retreated into self-centered fear and pride. Grandiosity and ignorance prompted us to think the answer was more — more food, money, sex, power — you name it. But trying to get more and more didn't work. In Step Seven we are asking a Higher Power to take over our lives and remove the shortcomings that prevent us from being of service to Him and to our fellow human beings. We're talking about *our* shortcomings. Not our boyfriend's laziness or our boss' temper, but *our* tendency to procrastinate and *our* self-righteous anger.

Often, the characteristics that annoy us about other people are the very same weaknesses we would rather not recognize in ourselves. We project our own shortcomings and see them as someone else's character defects. For example, we tend to be most critical of our children when we see in them some of the same negative traits that we exhibit in ourselves.

If we delude ourselves into thinking that our recovery depends on the behavior of the people with whom we live, or the external circumstances and events which affect our lives, we are putting ourselves in a bind. People and circumstances will never suit us perfectly. But we don't have to use that as an excuse to overeat and/or hang on to our own defects of character. Serenity and sanity come to us not when other people do what we want them to do, but when our first priority is to sincerely try to know and do God's will for us.

Growing pains

We ask God to remove the obsession with food over which we are powerless, and then we consider abstinence to be a gift from our Higher Power. For some of us, abstinence may come with relative ease once we completely surrender to the fact that when we take the first compulsive bite we are truly powerless over food. We come to accept that in order to grow up, we have to stop using excess food as a crutch. For others of us, abstinence may hurt for a while as our self-will and habits still struggle to retain control. (Self-will can masquerade as hunger, fatigue, fear, or any other rationale we use to prove that we are not compulsive overeaters.)

If we have to be uncomfortable for a period of time in order to learn how to face life without overeating, then so be it. The long-term freedom is well worth some temporary pain. Remember, none of us would choose to stay with an overeaters program if the pain of overeating were not far worse than whatever initial discomfort abstinence involved.

When we let go of our obsession with food, we begin to experience the peace and joy of being free from that compulsion. Humility is the key. As we become increasingly aware of our other liabilities besides compulsive overeating, we use the same Seventh Step key to open ourselves to the Power that frees us from these shortcomings, as well. But here, too, the process of growth may involve some short-term discomfort.

Our growing pains may be experienced as a series of waves,

like ocean waves which can overwhelm us with their immensity and power. By maintaining contact with our Higher Power, we learn to ride most of the waves. Every so often, one of the big ones might temporarily submerge us. But we know that it, too, will pass. The wave may knock us down. But through the program we are developing an inner core of peace that keeps us from being destroyed by fear or confusion.

When we tried to anesthetize ourselves with food to keep from feeling pain, our emotional and spiritual growth was arrested. God does not insulate us from hurt. Sometimes we have to feel pain in order to get better. What our Higher Power does is provide us with enough strength, faith, and inner peace to be able to roll with the punches and to learn the lessons contained in the unpleasant experiences. Pain is a teacher. It is a warning signal that we are off the track.

Like a splinter which needs to be removed or a tooth which needs to be pulled, our defects need to go. If we put our Higher Power in charge of recovery, we can recognize the pain of growth and know that it will not destroy us. In fact, growing pains are part of getting better.

Service

In the Seventh Step prayer quoted earlier, we asked God to remove our defects not only so we could be free of them, but also so we could be useful to Him and to our fellow human beings. When we were compulsively overeating, we were wrapped up in ourselves. Food was our god, and the idea of service was not a number-one priority. This is changing. As we live the new freedom and enthusiasm of abstinence, our gratitude for such a priceless gift makes us want to give in return.

The new life into which we are growing is one which is no longer self-centered. The more firmly we are grounded in a Higher Power, the better we feel and the more we want to be useful. We have learned that striving for material satisfaction does not work as a primary goal. We are discovering that happiness comes as a byproduct of seeking to know and follow God's will for our lives. We are not going to be perfect, but we can give to other people in spite of that. When we humbly put a Higher Power in charge of our renovation, we can relax and stop beating ourselves for our faults. God made us and is re-making us every day, and He doesn't make mistakes.

One of the reasons we were seeking the answer to life's questions in the refrigerator undoubtedly was because we had no workable, day-to-day, gut-level faith in a Power greater than ourselves. We may have believed in God, but we did not concretely apply that belief to our everyday thoughts and actions.

Now we are linked to a Power that makes a practical, fundamental difference in both the trivial and the significant events in our lives. We have found the strength and inspiration of an overeater's group, and the love and support of understanding individuals who want our strength, hope and love. An important part of our usefulness to God and our fellow human beings is what we give back to our group and what we share with family and friends outside the program.

Step Seven points the way to the freedom to be and do the best we can. The more we let ourselves be filled with the gifts our Higher Power has for us each day, the less room there will be for character defects. We pray simply and humbly for their removal. Then we can go about the business of the day, relying on God's grace to guide us, to fill our lives, and to overflow to those around us.